MW01445507

IT'S OFFICIAL!
YOU'RE THE OKAYEST!

AS YOUR REWARD FOR BEING OKAY, INSIDE YOU WILL FIND 20 MANDALAS FOR YOU TO SIT BACK AND COLOR

EACH ONE CONTAINS A COMPLIMENT THAT YOU REALLY HAVE EARNED FOR BEING THE OKAYEST

HAPPY COLORING!

COLORING CREW

COLORING CREW

COLORING CREW

COLORING CREW

COLORING CREW

COLORING CREW

COLORING CREW

COLORING
CREW

COLORING CREW

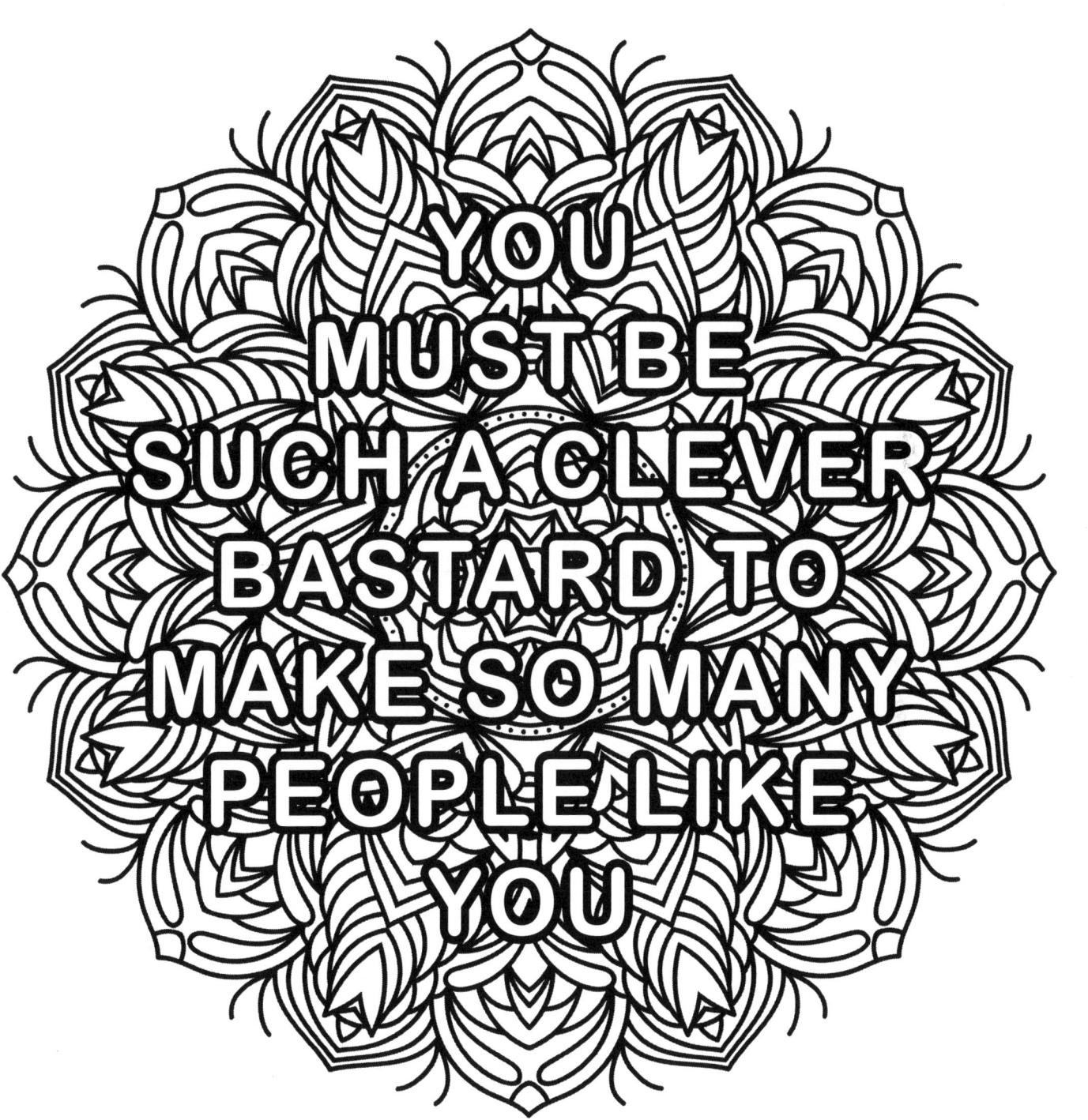

COLORING CREW

COLORING CREW

COLORING CREW

COLORING CREW

COLORING
CREW

COLORING CREW

COLORING
CREW

COLORING CREW

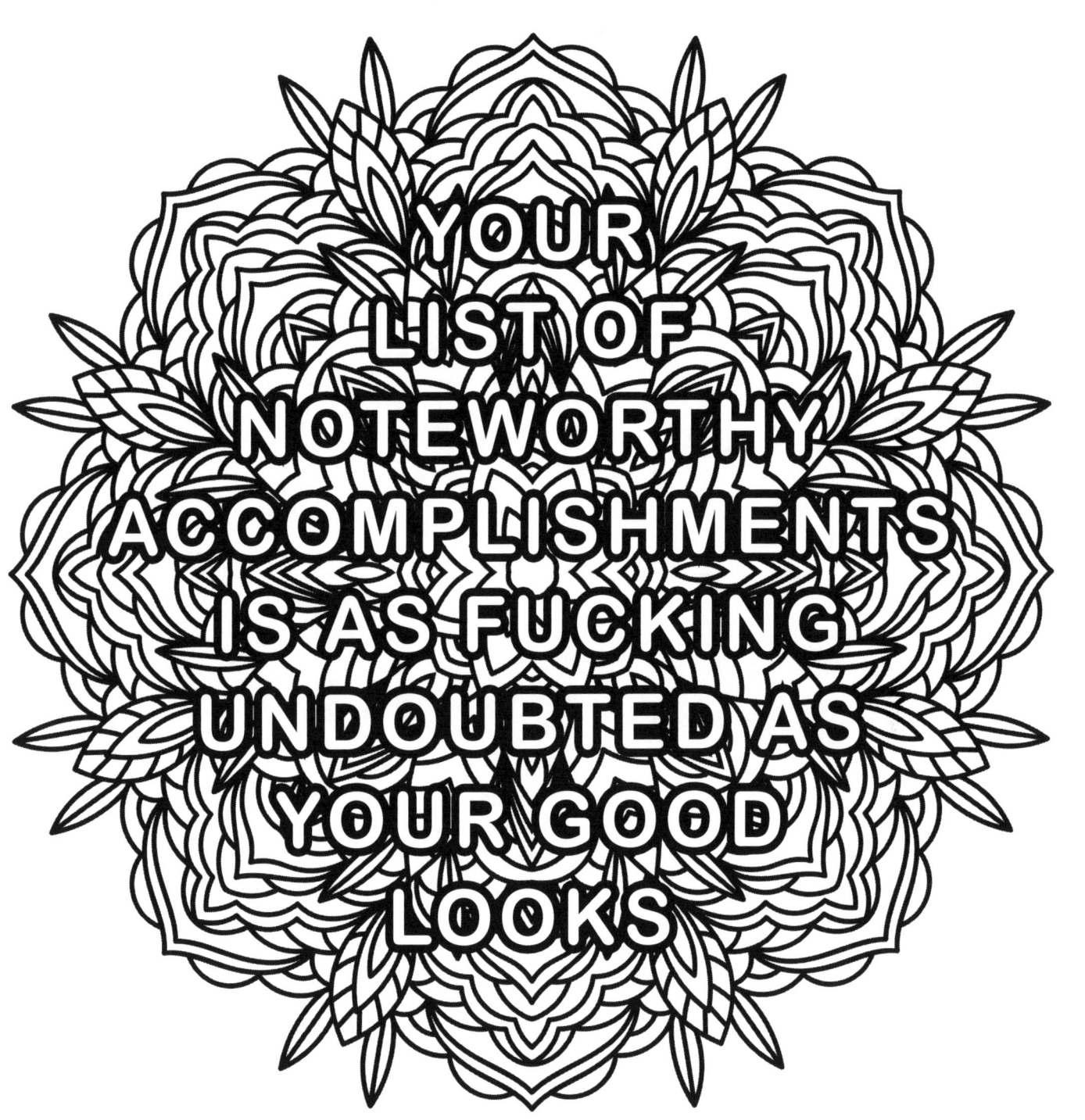

COLORING CREW

COLORING CREW

COLORING CREW

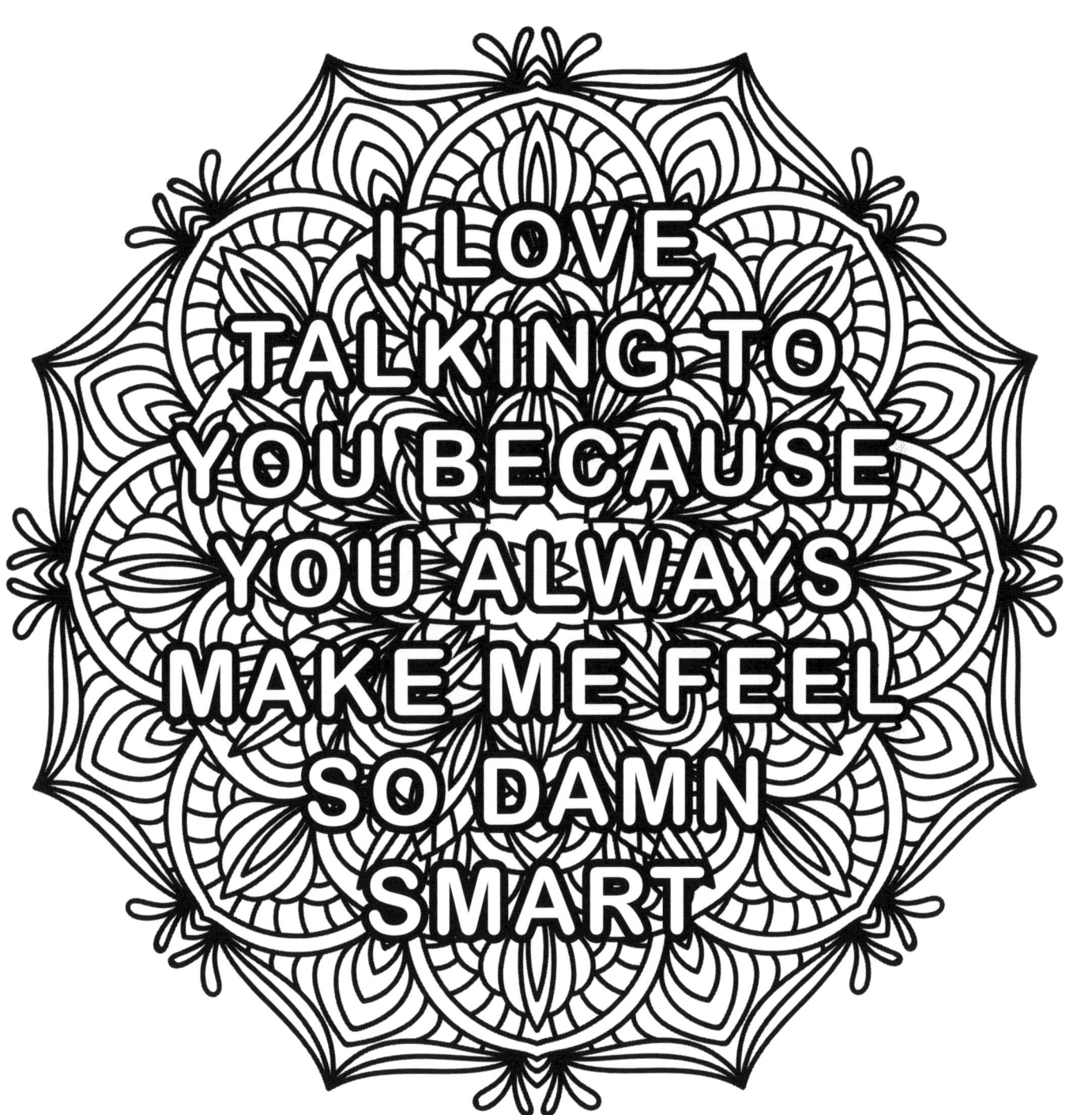

I LOVE TALKING TO YOU BECAUSE YOU ALWAYS MAKE ME FEEL SO DAMN SMART

COLORING CREW

COLOR TEST
PAGE

COLORING CREW

THANKS!
WE HOPE YOU HAD FUN!

IF YOU LIKED THIS BOOK THEN YOU YOU CAN
VIEW OUR FULL RANGE OF HILARIOUS ADULT
COLORING BOOKS BY GOING TO AMAZON AND
SEARCHING FOR "COLORING CREW" AND THEN
CLICKING ON OUR AUTHOR PAGE.

THANKS AGAIN!

COLORING CREW

Made in United States
Orlando, FL
05 April 2024